THE OLD WHITE HOUSE
...and other jokes!
VOLUME II

SWEET WATER PRESS

Birmingham, Alabama

THE CLINTON WHITE HOUSE

...and other jokes!

VOLUME II

What does President Clinton have in common with road kill?

No one wants to admit they are interested, but everyone takes the time to look at all the gory details.

What does President Clinton have in common with the space station Mir?

They've both been up longer than anyone expected and they both have a major incident every few months.

Did you hear about the new Bill Clinton computer operating system?

It goes down all the time, won't clarify errors, and won't admit damaging the system.

If Bill gets convicted, what should his sentence be?

Wife without parole!

Recently, Hillary visited a fortune teller. In a dark, hazy room, the mystic peered into a crystal ball and delivered some grave news.

"There's no easy way to say this, so I'll be blunt," the fortune teller said. "Prepare yourself for your husband to die a violent, horrible death this year."

Visibly shaken, Hillary took a few minutes to compose herself and ask a question:

"Will I be acquitted?"

During a visit to an elementary school, President Clinton said: "Today we are going to discuss the difference between a tragedy and a great loss. What's an example of a great loss?"

"A bus full of kids going off a cliff," said one little girl. Clinton asked for an example of tragedy.

"If you and Mrs. Clinton were on a plane and it blew up," said a little boy.

"Very good," said Clinton. "But why is that a tragedy?"

The boy replied: "Well, it wouldn't be a great loss!"

Clinton finds a bottle and opens it. A genie pops out and grants him one wish. Clinton wishes for peace in the Middle East. The genie says there are some things even a genie can't do and tells Clinton to make another wish. Clinton says he wishes the whole Monica thing would go away. The genie says he'll take a second look at the map of the Middle East.

Who owns the most famous cigar box
in history?

Monica Lewinsky.

Bill and Hillary are at a restaurant. The waiter tells them tonight's specials are almond chicken and fresh fish.

"The chicken sounds good," says Hillary. "I'll have that."

The waiter asks, "And the vegetable?"

"Oh, he'll have the fish," Hillary replies.

Reagan, Bush, and Clinton
are on the *Titanic*.
Reagan says, "Save the women!"
Bush says, "Screw the women!"
Clinton says, "Do we have time?!"

★ ★ ★ ★ ★ ★ ★

What is the difference between
George Washington, Richard Nixon,
and Bill Clinton?
Washington couldn't tell a lie,
Nixon couldn't tell the truth, and
Clinton doesn't know the difference.

Dr. Joycelyn Elders was talking with some friends about the easiest people to operate on. One surgeon said engineers were easiest because their insides are color-coded. Another surgeon said librarians are easiest because their insides are arranged in alphabetical order. Elders said Clinton is by far the easiest: He has no guts, no spine, no heart, and his sexual organs and brain are interchangeable!

Sunday morning, Chief of Staff Erskine Bowles approached the president. "Mr. President, I am afraid I have some bad news, some good news, and some bad news for you."

"Give it to me in order," requested the President.

"The bad news is that a picket demanding your impeachment is in front of the White House," said Bowles. "The good news is that there's only one person so far."

"What's so bad about that," asked the President.

"Well," Bowles said, "it's Gore holding the sign."

The president got a dog so Hillary wouldn't be confused when she walked past the Oval Office and heard, "Roll over. Sit. Stay. Good. Now here's your bone."

The Secret Service got a real scare the other day when someone threw a beer at President Clinton during his morning jog.

Fortunately, it was a draft, so he was able to dodge it.

In a spelling contest between
Sen. Ted Kennedy, Dan Quayle,
Sen. Bob Packwood, and Bill Clinton,
who would win?

Dan Quayle—he's the only one who
knows that *harass* is one word.

What are the two worst things about
Bill Clinton?

His faces.

While the First Family vacationed at Camp David
the housekeeper looked after their pet parrot.
Unfortunately the parrot died.

The housekeeper set out to find a replacement. After two days,
she found one—a parrot that had lived for several years
in a house of ill repute.

The morning after the Clintons returned to the White House,
Chelsea walked through the room and the bird said,
"Too young."

A little later Hillary came into the room and the bird responded
with, "Too old."

Late that afternoon the president entered the room and
the bird said, "HI, BILL!"

★ ★ ★ ★ ★ ★ ★

President Clinton steps off Air Force One
carrying a small dog.

"Nice dog, sir," said a Secret Service
man.

"Thanks," Clinton said. "I got it for
Hillary."

"Nice trade, sir!"

President Clinton looked out onto the White House lawn in the dead of winter and saw "Impeach the President" written in urine on the snow.

Clinton ordered the Secret Service to find out who did it. Later that evening, his chief security officer approached him: "Well, Mr. President, we have some bad news and we have some really bad news."

"Give me the bad news first," Clinton said.

"The urine belonged to Al Gore."

"Well, what's the really bad news?"

"It's Hillary's handwriting."

Clinton didn't commit adultery with Monica Lewinsky.

She wasn't an adult.

★ ★ ★ ★ ★ ★ ★

President and Mrs. Clinton are at a baseball game. As the game is about to start, Bill stands up, picks up Hillary, and throws her out onto the field. When he sits down, his chief advisor leans over and says, "You know, Bill, you may have misunderstood me. I said you have to throw out the first *pitch*."

Why is Monica always on top?
Bill can only screw up.

A friend asked President Clinton if he ever talked to Hillary while making love.

Clinton replied: "She calls me on the phone a lot, so that happens."

I just got a new Bill Clinton doll. Have you heard about them?

Pull the string and it never says the same thing twice.

Elementary school teacher: We're going to take a special quiz today, class. A correct answer means you can go home for the day. Who said, "Give me liberty or give me death"?

Schoolgirl #1: Patrick Henry.

Teacher: That's right. See you tomorrow. Who said, "Ask not what your country can do for you, but what you can do for your country"? ...

... Schoolgirl #2: John F. Kennedy.

Teacher: That's right.
You can go home, too.

Schoolboy: Stupid girls should keep
their mouths shut.

Teacher: Who said that?

Schoolboy: Bill Clinton.
See you tomorrow.

What do Monica Lewinsky and a vending machine have in common?

Both say "Insert Bill here.

Bill and Hillary were strolling in front of the White House one day and met a boy giving away puppies. When Hillary said they were cute, the little boy said, "Yes, ma'am, they are. They're Democrats."

"Oh, how sweet," Hillary said. "If you have any left next weekend I'll take one."

That Sunday, Bill and Hillary again saw the little boy, who had two puppies left.

"Only two left ma'am," the boy said. "And they're both Republicans."

"But the other day you said they were Democrats," Hillary said.

"Well, yes ma'am, but since then they've opened their eyes."

33

Hillary Clinton went in for a checkup and learned she was pregnant. She angrily dialed the Oval Office. When Bill answered, Hillary said: "You got me pregnant!"

The president remained quiet.

Again, Hillary screamed: "DO YOU KNOW WHAT YOU DID? YOU GOT ME PREGNANT!!!"

Finally Bill answered, "Who is this???"

What do Lucille Ball and Monica Lewinsky have in common?

They've both enjoyed a Cuban.

While jogging one morning, Bill Clinton stopped
at the Washington monument to ask:
"George, what should I do?"

George replied, "Abolish the IRS and start over."

Bill thought about this as he continued jogging.
When he reached the Jefferson Memorial he said,
"Tom, what should I do?"

Tom replied, "Abolish welfare and start over."

Bill continued jogging to the Lincoln Memorial. He said,
"Abe, what should I do?"

Abe replied, "Why don't you take the night off
and go to the theater?"

Clinton received a letter from a man threatening to break his legs if he bothered his wife one more time.

Clinton consulted with Vernon Jordan, who suggested the president contact the man and promise never to see his wife again.

"I can't," Clinton said. "The guy didn't sign his name."

The Secret Service code word
for the stain on the blue dress is
"Presidue."

How can Clinton save his presidency?

Hit more home runs than Mark McGwire and Sammy Sosa.

What's the difference between Al Gore and Leonardo DiCaprio?

Al Gore's actually on a sinking ship.

Did you know the Clinton Presidential
Library has already been built?

It's every adult bookstore
in Little Rock.

Clinton Stew:
one small weenie
in a lot of hot water.

What was Monica's last gift to Bill?

An autographed picture of the top
of her head.

Monica allegedly told Kenneth Starr
that she merely wanted someone
she could look up to.

What's the difference between Monica's blue dress and Bill Clinton?

The blue dress will eventually come clean.

What is Monica's favorite song?
"Devil with a Blue Dress"

What does Sen. Ted Kennedy have that
Bill Clinton wishes HE did?

A dead girlfriend.

Why does the Secret Service guard
Hillary so closely?

If something happens to her
Bill becomes president.

What did Boris Yeltsin say when asked whether meeting President Clinton made him want to convert Russia to the type of government America has?

"Heck no, I'm not letting my wife run the country."

What did Ronald Reagan say after
hearing President Clinton's State
of the Union speech?

"You know, Nancy, the man is a better
actor than I ever was."

What does Bill Clinton have in common
with a discount store?

They both have lingerie half off!

What's the difference between Bill Clinton and Santa Claus?

Some people still believe in Santa Claus.

What's the difference between Clinton and a whale?

Whales mate for life.

What's the difference between Bill Clinton and a container of yogurt?

Yogurt has culture.

How do you spot Bill Clinton in a room full of Secret Service agents?

He's the stiff one.

What were the three toughest years in
Bill Clinton's life?

Sixth grade.

If Hillary Clinton gets health care,
Lloyd Bentsen gets treasury,
and William Cohen gets defense,
what does Al Gore get?

Coffee.

What is Clinton's plan to create thousands of small businesses?

Take thousands of big businesses and wait four years.

What is the first thing President Clinton says after waking up?

"Good morning, Bill."

Two new interns are hired in the White House. As they are walking down the hall, President Clinton walks up and says, "Gee, I've never come across your faces before."

When did Clinton's friends become sure
he had political ambitions?

When he married outside of his family.

How can you identify a computer that has been used at the Clinton White House?

There is correction fluid on the screen.

Former Vice President Dan Quayle, Speaker of the House Newt Gingrich, and President Bill Clinton were traveling by car in the Midwest. A tornado suddenly whirled them into the air and dumped them in the land of Oz.

The trio went off to see the Wizard.

Dan Quayle stepped forward and said: "I would very much like to have a brain."

Newt Gingrich stepped forward to say: "I would very much like to have a heart."

President Clinton glanced left and right, then asked, "Where's Dorothy?"

What do you call Monica Lewinsky
with a runny nose?

Full.

President Clinton, Vice President Al Gore, and Hillary Clinton all died the same day.

God said to Bill, "You were the leader of the free world. Sit here, on my right side."

God then turned to Al Gore and said, "You were the assistant leader of the free world. Sit here, on my left side."

God then turned to Hillary, but before he could say a word, Hillary shouted: "I'm Hillary Clinton, and you're sitting in my seat!"

What did Clinton say when asked if he had used protection?

"Sure, there was a guard standing right outside the door."

Just before a meeting with Vice President Al Gore, President Clinton learned the FBI would be able to identify the stains on Monica's cocktail dress by obtaining hair, saliva, or blood samples.

The meeting opened as follows:

Clinton: Hi, Al, have a seat. I wanted to talk about . . . hey, do you know your hair is sticking up in back? Here, use my hairbrush . . .

Who were Monica's two best friends
while she was at the White House?

Neil and Bob.

★ ★ ★ ★ ★ ★ ★

"It all started out innocently," Monica Lewinsky exclaimed to the throng of reporters outside the courthouse where she testified before the grand jury. "Bill kept saying he was taking me to the Oval Office to look at his clock. When we got there, he dropped his drawers. 'That's not a clock,' I told him. And he said, 'so put two hands and a face on it and we'll pretend!'"

What's the difference between
John F. Kennedy and Bill Clinton?

One had his head blown off. The other
was assassinated.

What's the difference between George Washington and Bill Clinton?

George Washington was the father of our country. Bill Clinton is the father of your grandchildren.

What's the difference between
Teddy Roosevelt and Bill Clinton?

They both walked softly but Clinton had
someone else take care of his big stick.

To the American people, Bill Clinton is the Commander-in-Chief.

To Monica Lewinsky, he is the Commander-in-Cheek.

Bill Clinton dies on his birthday and is whisked away to stand before the pearly gates. Saint Peter peers intently at his computer screen with an eyebrow raised.

"Looks like you've had a thing for the young ladies, Bill."

Clinton swallows the lump in his throat.

After a long pause, Saint Peter says, "But I see you finally settled down and behaved yourself for the past year or so."

The gates swing open, and Clinton is motioned inside.

"By the way," Saint Peter adds, "Congratulations on your birthday. Not many people make it to a hundred and ten."

Now Monica has that glamorous
advertising job she's always wanted.
In her first television spot, she smiles
as she uses a Water Pik and says,
"It gets into places even the President
can't reach!"

Monica's dress will be known in history as "the spot heard round the world."

Monica was planning on getting a new dress but she decided to stick to the one she has.

How do you get on Bill Clinton's good side?

Suck up!

When Bill Clinton was asked about his favorite advertising slogan, he replied "JUST DO IT."

Why did Bill Clinton cross the road?

To get back to the White House
before Hillary did.

Hillary Clinton wakes in the middle of the night. She shakes Bill to wake him up.

Hillary: Bill, Bill, wake up.

Bill keeps sleeping.

Hillary: Bill, Bill, wake up!

Bill finally wakes up and groggily says: What do you want?

Hillary: I have to use the bathroom.

Bill: Well then why did you wake me up?

Hillary: I wanted to tell you to save my spot.

What warning does Clinton give interns
when they leave his office?

"Mind you don't hit your head
on the desk!"

Clinton was watching the
Miss Teen USA pageant on television
the other night. What did he think
he was watching?

The Home Shopping Network!

Monica just got her first acting job!
She's a stunt double in the
milk commercials.

What do Monica and a hurricane
have in common?

Both blow hard and leave a mess.

Hillary Clinton arrives at Saint Peter's gate, and sees a wall covered with clocks. She asks why there are clocks in eternity. Saint Peter explains that every time someone commits adultery his or her clock ticks forward.

Hillary asks to see her husband's clock.

Saint Peter says, "Because your husband is President of the United States he has the grandest clock of all, but you can't see it because God keeps it in his bedroom to use as a fan."

There's a new Bill Clinton computer coming out soon.

It will have a six-inch hard drive, but no memory.

President Clinton fell into the Potomac and was saved by a little boy.

"You were very brave," Clinton said. "I'm going to grant you three wishes."

"I want twenty pounds of candy."

Clinton agrees.

"I want to take my family to the Grand Canyon." ...

... Again, Clinton agrees.

"And I want to be buried in Arlington National Cemetery."

"I understand the first two," Clinton says. "But why the third?"

"When I tell my daddy I saved your life, he's gonna kill me!"

Did you hear that Monica Lewinsky
coughed up new evidence?

★ ★ ★ ★ ★ ★ ★

After surgery, Monica asked, "How soon will I be able to resume a normal sex life?"

"Oh, it won't be long," replied the doctor, looking puzzled.

"Why do you look so surprised," asked Monica.

"Well," replied the doctor, "to be perfectly honest, I've never had a tonsillectomy patient ask me that question before!"

Don't miss the movie *Primary Colors*.
It stars John Travolta as Bill Clinton,
Emma Thompson as Hillary Clinton, and
Monica Lewinsky as the beaver.

What did Monica say when she finally met Hillary?

"I'll huff and I'll puff until I blow your husband ... down."

What did Kenneth Starr say when he
finally met Hillary?

The same thing.

The White House scandal wasn't really President Clinton's fault, it was just something he got sucked into.

Did you hear that President Clinton is supporting a new math curriculum in the nation's schools?

He wants everyone to know that fifty can go into twenty-one without getting five to ten.

What's the worst thing Bill Clinton ever heard during sex?

"Honey, I'm home!!"

How did President Clinton create fourteen million new jobs during his administration?

Thirteen million of them are comedians.

When Bill Clinton walks into a room,
the band plays "Tail to the Chief."

Finally, a Bush has defeated Clinton.

What does Bill tell Hillary after sex?
Nothing. She hears about it on the evening news!

What does Clinton like more than roses on his piano?

Tulips on his organ.

If Monica was a bird, what kind would she be?

A swallow.

Why can't Monica become a spy?

Because she spits everything out when the debriefing's done.

When asked what she thought of President Clinton's State of the Union address, Monica replied: "I'll give it two legs up!"

What's Clinton's favorite mountain range?

The Himalayas.

Did you hear Clinton doesn't use bookmarks?

He just bends over the pages!

★ ★ ★ ★ ★ ★ ★

Clinton and the Pope died on the same day, but due to an administrative error, Clinton was sent to heaven and the Pope was sent to hell. Satan straightened out the situation, but the Pope had to wait twenty-four hours for the error to be corrected.

The next day, as the Pope was on his way to heaven he ran into President Clinton, who was on his way down.

Pope: Sorry about the mix up, but I'm really excited about going to heaven.

Clinton: Why is that?

Pope: All my life I've wanted to meet the Virgin Mary.

Clinton: Sorry, you're a day late.

I was a White House intern and all I got
was this stain on my T-shirt.

★ ★ ★ ★ ★ ★ ★

How do you know when you've had a lunch date with the President?

You've got fries in your hair, a stain on your dress, and your mouth is full of Whopper!

Is the President having sex with
Tipper Gore?

No, but by this time next year she might
be having sex with the president.

Did you hear about the new charge being brought against Clinton?

Using an intern as a humidor.